Native American Heritage™ Series

Native American Big Activity Book

Native American Biographies

Native American Coloring Book

Native American Heritage Book

Native American Timeline

Colorado STATE STUFF™

I0892159

- My First Pocket Guide: Colorado
- My First Book About Colorado
- Colorado Coloring Book
- The Big Colorado Reproducible Activity Book
- Jeopardy: Answers & Questions About Our State
- Colorado "Jography!": A Fun Run Through Our State
- Colorado Gamebooks
- Colorado Bingo Games
- Colorado Illustrated Timelines
- Colorado Project Books
- Colorado Bulletin Board Set
- Colorado PosterMap
- Colorado Stickers
- Let's Discover Colorado! CD-ROM

Word from the Author

Hello!

I hope you are as interested in North America's wonderful Indian heritage as I am!

Like most kids, I grew up thinking of Indians as the other half of Cowboys. Today, of course, we are getting a much clearer and more accurate picture of what the first peoples on our land were all about. These "facts" are much more fascinating than anything Hollywood can make up. And you probably won't find much of this information in your history textbook!

I am 1/16 Cherokee. This is something I am very proud of and happy about. My grandmother was 1/4 Cherokee. She had tan skin, long gray hair and a very Indian look – especially if I did something bad! Her maiden name was Carrie Corn. Of course, when she got married, she took her husband's name, so it was many years before I learned to appreciate the significance of my native heritage.

Today, I'm trying to make up for lost time by exploring my roots as deeply as I can. One of the most interesting things I've learned is how fascinating all of the Indian tribes are – in the past, the present and future!

As you read about "your" Indians, remember that all native peoples were part of an ever-changing network of time, ideas, power and luck — good and bad. This is certainly a history that is not "dead," but continues to change – often right outside our own back doors! – all the time.

Carole Marsh
She-Who-Writes

PS: Many references show different spellings for the same word. I have tried to select the most common spelling for the time period described. I would not want to be in an Indian spelling bee!

A is for . . .

Adobe

Brick made of mud plus straw and dried in the sun. Houses made of adobe are cool inside, even in high temperatures, because the walls are so thick.

Arapaho

Famous raiding tribe of Plains Indians. Had horses and hunted buffalo. Noted for their beadwork. Observed the Sun Dance. Brave and warlike. Lived with and intermarried with the Cheyenne, but never learned their language and kept their own customs.

Adze

An Indian woodworking tool used to cut, scrape, or gouge; often used to hollow dugout canoes. Blades were made of stone, shell, bone or copper.

Anasazi

Early Colorado people who lived at Mesa Verde. Name means "the ancient ones." They made beautiful pottery, dammed streams, grew corn, squash, beans and gourds, and traded with distant tribes for salt, turquoise and cotton. Since their paintings do not show warfare, they probably lived in peace with their neighbors. Around 1300, they disappeared. They resettled in what today is New Mexico and Arizona. Their descendants are the Pueblo Indians.

Antelope

Used as food and for clothing by Colorado Indians. Buckskin was used for moccasin tops and vests, hair for pillow and mattress stuffing, shinbones for pipes and horns for tools.

Altar

A platform made of rocks or animal skulls; some had bowls, feathers, rattles, or skins on them. Indians prayed at these altars for things like good crops or expert hunting skills.

Arrow

A long, slender shaft made of reed, cane, or wood; pointed tip was attached to one end and split feathers to the other. Feathers helped the arrows fly straight.

Arrowhead

The pointed tip of an arrow, made of bone, antler, wood, or iron. Some tips had barbs that would embed themselves in flesh. These barbs made it difficult for an enemy to remove the arrowhead from a wound.

Aborigine

A member of the earliest known population of a region.

Apache

In the early 1600s, roamed southeastern Colorado. They heard that newcomers with pale skin had settled in the southern mountains, and rode on the backs of large beasts. Some of the warriors captured these animals — the horse. Soon, Apache were expert riders, traded horses, and even moved to the deserts of the south.

B is for . . .

Basketmakers

Around A.D. 1, archaeologists say that these people lived in caves at Mesa Verde in southwestern Colorado. They wove baskets so tightly, they could carry water! They probably traded with peoples from the Gulf coast of the U.S., because they made jewelry using shells from that area.

Band

A subdivision of an Indian tribe. In earlier times, a band was sometimes created when part of a tribe split off from the main group. The band also chose new leadership.

Blankets

Used for door covers, partitions, bags, to dry food on, carry babies and many other purposes.

Bent's Fort

Trading post built in 1833 near todays La Junta. William Bent married a Cheyenne chief's daughter. He won the respect of the Cheyenne and the Arapahoes who brought their buffalo robes here to trade.

Buffalo

Made up the major diet of many Indian tribes. Hides were used as blankets or tents. Every tribe member was given a piece of the animal to eat. There were strict rules about not hunting buffalo alone, so that one person wouldn't scare them all away! To catch the animals, the hunters chased them off cliffs or encircled them in fire, then shot them.

Bannock

Shoshonean-speaking, nomadic tribe that ranged into parts of Colorado after the early 1700s. Foraged for food, but after acquiring the horse they hunted for buffalo.

Bow

Made from wood, horn or bone. Colorado Indian children learned how to use bows. The bowstring was made from animal gut, rawhide or twisted vegetable fibers.

Battle of Summit Springs

1869; marked the end of the Indian wars in eastern Colorado.

Beads

Made of wood, shells, claws, minerals, seeds — you name it! Later, the Colorado Indians traded with white men for glass beads, used in some of their decorative arts.

C is for . . .

Chief

Leader of a tribe. Different titles meant different things. Some members were made chief because they owned deeds to land. Chieftainship was often inherited, usually from the mother!

Contact Period

What historians call the era in the 1500s when Native Americans first met Europeans. This meeting changed the lifestyle of the Colorado Indians more than anyone could ever have anticipated!

Comanche

Famous Indian tribe of the Plains. Expert horsemen. Famous horse breeders and trainers with huge herds. Buffalo hunters and warlike. Roamed much of the Plains, including Colorado, in the 1700 and 1800s. Eventually forced to live on a reservation in Oklahoma.

Cheyenne

Famous tribe of Plains Indians. Allied with the Arapaho. Powerful, athletic, smart, brave. Horse Indians and buffalo hunters. Lived in tepees. Warlike—one of the most important players in the Indian conflicts on the Great Plains. The Southern Cheyenne could be found in eastern Colorado after the early 1830s. The Southern Cheyenne were forced to a reservation in Indian Territory in the late 1860s.

Confederacy

A union of different groups of people. A confederacy in Indian culture was a group of tribes that agreed not to fight with each other. They agreed to live peacefully. Sometimes the tribes shared culture and language.

Chimney Rock

Anasazi site once occupied by as many as 2,000 people. There are still 100 unexcavated mounds in this area.

Clan

A tribal unit. Members are descended from the same ancestor.

Cliff Dwellers

Bands of nomadic hunters and gatherers who wandered over Colorado's mountains and plains nearly 2,000 years ago. They hunted buffalo and moved around in search of food, never stopping to plant crops.

Classic Pueblo Period

By 1100 A.D., early people of southwestern Colorado lived prosperously. They lived in large towns or pueblos built into the cliffs. Many one-room houses were joined to form great "apartment buildings" three to four stories high.

Cliff Palace

Mesa Verde pueblo that contained more than 200 one-room dwellings.

D is for . . .

Dance

There were Indian dances for every occasion: war, peace, hunting, rain, good harvests, etc. Drums, rattles, and flutes of bone or reed provided the music. Dancers often chanted or sang while performing. Steps were not easy to learn and required consistent practice.

Descendants

The first Colorado Indians were descendants of primitive hunters who crossed the Bering Strait from Asia to what is now Alaska. At that time, glacial ice still covered most of North America. These people were the true discoverers of the "New World!"

Disease

Colorado Indians had no immunity to the diseases that white explorers, colonists and settlers brought to their lands. These diseases included smallpox, measles, tuberculosis and others, which ravaged the tribes in great epidemics that killed many, and sometimes all, members of a tribe.

Denver Art Museum

Here you can see Indian art, costumes, pottery, textiles, kachinas, silverwork, blankets, baskets and much more in one of the world's finest collections of Native American artworks.

Dyes

Made of lichens, berries, roots, bark, plants, and other natural materials by Indians in Colorado. Different colors were used depending on what materials were available and what objects were to be dyed.

Decisions, Decisions!

The Cheyenne had a special council - the Council of Forty-four. Each of the 44 Cheyenne bands had a peace chief, who was on the council. They settled disputes, decided when to move, made tribal war policy decisions and decisions on alliances with other tribes.

Dishes

Made from clay, bark, wood, stone, and other materials, depending on what was available and what food they would be used for.

Dreams

Important in the Indian tradition. It was believed that dreams were the "windows" to the soul. Many thought a person's hidden desires were expressed in dreams.

E is for . . .

Eagle

An animal used in many Indian ceremonies. Eagle feathers attached to war bonnets and shields communicated an Indian's rank in his tribe and what kinds of deeds he had done. Feathers also adorned rattles, pipes, baskets, and prayer sticks.

Enjoy Visits to These Colorado Indian Museums

Anasazi Heritage Center, Dolores; Buffalo Bill Memorial Museum, Golden; Colorado History Museum, Denver; El Pueblo History Museum, Pueblo; Koshare Museum, La Junta; Manitou Cliff Dwellings Museum, Manitou; Mesa Verde National Park Museum, Mesa Verde National Park; Southern Ute Indian Cultural Center, Ignacio; Ute Indian Museum, Montrose; Ute Mountain Tribal Park, Towaoc.

Earrings

Medicine men sometimes pierced male and female ears at special ceremonies. Earrings, which cost parents or relatives a significant amount, symbolized wealth and distinction. The more earrings that an Indian wore, the greater his honor. Some earrings measured 12 inches in length!

Escalante Ruin

Near Dolores; first recorded prehistoric site in Colorado; see 9 rooms, a kiva and midden that date back to A.D. 900-1300.

El Cuartelejo

Possibly once located in eastern Colorado. In the 1690s, Pueblo slaves fled from Sante Fe and found shelter with the Apaches here.

English

In the 1800s, the U.S. government built boarding schools for Indian children throughout the nation. Children were forced to leave their homes and families to live at these schools. They were required to learn English and not speak their native languages.

Epidemics

Few Indians possessed immunity to the deadly diseases, like smallpox and measles, which European explorers and settlers brought to the New World. As a result, great population loss took place. Sometimes entire tribes became extinct. Epidemics sparked by Hernando De Soto's expedition are estimated to have killed 75% of the native population in the New World.

F is for . . .

Fort Vasquez

Where Indians traded buffalo robes for ivory combs!

Fetish

These small objects were thought to hold the spirit of an animal or a part of nature. A fetish could be an object found in nature, such as bone or wood, or it could be a carved object. The fetish was usually small enough to be carried in a small bag or on a cord. The making and use of a fetish was kept secret by its owner and only shared with the one who inherited it.

Fishers

Early Colorado peoples hunted and gathered to keep from starving. Later, they learned to fish. When they finally learned to farm crops, they were more able to settle down into villages, instead of needing to forage all the time.

Fire Drill

A device used by Indians to make fires which consisted of a stick and a piece of wood with a tight hole in it. The stick was twirled rapidly in the hole, creating friction that would ignite shredded grass or wood powder placed nearby to start a fire.

Farmers

Many Colorado Indians, ancient and modern, have farming ways! Even pre-contact Indians tilled and irrigated, raising many important crops. Corn, cotton, beans, squash, melons, sunflowers, gourds, pumpkins and tobacco are all native Indian crops!

Federal Recognition

The United States government's official acknowledgement of a group of Indians as a tribe that is eligible for government benefits, programs and funds.

Footwear

Colorado Indians wore different footwear depending on their tribe and environment. Moccasins were made mostly of animal skin. Sandals were made of rawhide or plant material.

Fort Laramie Treaty

The first of two treaties signed here, the one in 1851, gave Southern Cheyenne and Arapaho tribes joint control over a large buffalo range between the South Platte and Arkansas Rivers. The treaty also promised lands to the Sioux, Crow, Assiniboine, and Gros Ventre. The promise to the Cheyenne and Arapaho was later ignored when gold was discovered on their reservation.

G is for . . .

Games

Adults played ball and other games of chance or skill. Indian children spun tops, fought pretend battles, did target-shooting, walked on stilts, played hide and seek, or competed to see who could hold their breath the longest!

Gold

The discovery of gold on the western fringe of the Cheyenne and Arapaho reservation brought great tension between whites and Indians. Older chiefs wanted to keep peace, even though the U. S. government had reduced their reservation to a small area. But younger warriors carried on raids anyway! The Utes were also pressured into signing away their gold-bearing lands for a reservation.

Gens

Group of related members from different tribes.

Gathering

Native Americans gathered natural materials for food, fuel, baskets, clothing, and housing. American Indians tribes also hunted to meet basic needs. Even though some tribes planted crops, most did some kind of gathering.

Gorgets

Beautiful ornaments hung around the neck or from ears; their significance, if any, is unknown.

Gourds

Hollowed-out shell of a gourd plant's dried fruit which often grew into a specific shape. Indians raised many species of gourds. They were used for spoons, bowls, masks, rattles, and even storage.

Go To These Exciting Indian Events in Our State

Annual Fellowship Pow-Wow – February, Greeley; Annual Denver March Pow Wow – March, Denver; Annual Hozhoni Days Powwow – March, Durango; NCIPA Annual Spring Powwow and Indian Market – April, Loveland; Annual Southern Ute Bear Dance Contest Powwow – May, Ignacio; Ute Mountain Ute Bear Dance Pow-Wow – June, Towaoc; Annual Sacred Gatherings Pow Wow – July, Larkspur/ Monument; Southern Ute Fair Powwow – September, Ignacio; Annual Council Tree Pow Wow and Cultural Festival – September, Delta.

H is for . . .

Horn and Hooves

Indians used animal horn to make spoons and dishes. Hooves were made into rattles and bird beaks were used for decoration.

Hatchet

A small, short-handled ax, primarily used as a tool, not as a weapon. When settlers moved in, stone hatchets were replaced with iron ones.

Headman

Apache leader of a band, chosen for leadership abilities and military prowess.

Hair

Indians used hair as a textile. Hair from bison, mountain sheep, elk, moose, deer, dog, rabbit, beaver, or even humans were used to weave cloth, make wigs, or stuff pillows, balls, dolls or drumsticks.

Hunters

Early Indian peoples were hunters who used wooden spears with stone points to kill many kinds of large mammals that are extinct today, such as mammoths and mastodons!

Hear the Message!

The Ghost Dance Religion spread among the Plains Tribes in the 1880s. It centered around returning to native ways and living together in harmony. It preached that the earth would soon die, to come alive again for only the Indians. The religion called for ridding oneself of the white ways, prayer, meditation, chanting and dancing – particularly the Ghost Dance. Although the founder of the religion was Paiute, the Arapaho wrote most of the Ghost Dance songs.

Hovenweep National Monument

Near Cortez; Hovenweep means "deserted valley." The Anasazi moved here and six village sites can still be visited here.

Horses

Spaniards brought the horse to America. At first, Indians were afraid of the horse or thought it was sacred. Later, Indians "broke" horses gently, often "hypnotizing" them with a blanket. Horses were used for transportation, trade, barter or paymenl. Some Indians ate horse meat in hopes of gaining the animal's power.

I is for . . .

Indian Scout

This term for a guide applied to Indians or white-skinned people who served that role.

Indian Reservation

A tract of land set aside by a government for Indians to live on.

Indian Removal Act of 1830

This federal act gave President Andrew Jackson the power to relocate tribes east of the Mississippi to an "Indian Territory." The forced removal of the southeast Indians later became known as the "Trail of Tears."

Independence

Native American tribes are sovereign nations. That means they are independent. Some even issue their own passports! However, Native Americans are also considered citizens of the United States and enjoy all the rights and privileges of U.S. citizens.

Indian Wars in Colorado

Some include: 1863-1869 war against the Cheyenne, Arapaho, Kiowa and Comanche; 1878 Ute expedition; 1915 Paiute War.

Indian

In 1493, Christopher Columbus called the native people he met in North America "Indians" because he mistakenly believed he had sailed to India! Today, this term includes the aborigines of North and South America.

Indian Ladder

Indians made ladders by trimming branches off a tree. Some were left at consistent intervals to provide steps.

Indian Tribes in Colorado

At one time or another, these tribes have lived in the state of Colorado:

Apache, Arapaho, Bannock, Comanche, Navajo, Ute

J is for . . .

Just So You Know . . .

Today you can find many Colorado Indians that follow some traditional ways. But there are also many who are entrepreneurs, doctors, lawyers, educators and even politicians! If you visit a reservation or cultural event, make sure you know visitor etiquette. Often dances are religious ceremonies and should be observed as such; religious dances should not be applauded. Photography, videotaping and drawing are all important issues - check with the tribe or individual before any is started.

Justice?

For hundreds of years, Native Americans have not received justice from federal and state governments. Native Americans have had nearly all their land taken away. Native Americans still have to fight for their rights in courts across the land.

Jicarilla

The Jicarilla Apache were buffalo hunters and lived in the Plains Indian style. At one time, Colorado was part of their territory.

Judicial Termination

Modern term to describe current efforts by various U.S. government agencies and officials (especially the judicial system) to legally decrease the sovereignty of independent Indian tribes.

Jerked Meat

Thin strips of buffalo, elk, deer or other animal meat which is dried on racks in the sun; also called "jerky."

Just In Time!

The Indian Arts and Crafts Act of 1990 makes it against the law to pretend that an item has been made by Native Americans if it is really not. It is illegal to offer or display for sale, or sell any art or craft product in a way that falsely suggests it is Indian produced.

K is for . . .

Kiva

Hopi Indian term for a circular chamber, usually underground, used for ceremonies.

Kiowa

Warlike tribe that once ranged in Colorado. Dark-skinned and stocky. Horse Indians and buffalo hunters. Today live on a reservation in Oklahoma.

Kiowa Legend

The Great Spirit once planted a tree that reached up to heaven. All of the animals of the plain climbed down from its branches to earth. The last to come down were a Kiowa man and woman. At the base of the tree, they met a buffalo. The Great Spirit told them, "The buffalo will be your food and clothes, but the day you see them perish from the earth, you will know that the end of the Kiowa is near and the sun is set." When white settlers came and the buffalo were killed off, this legend became partly true—it was the end of their way of life.

Killed Pottery

Pottery placed in a grave as an offering to the dead person was called killed pottery. A hole was formed in its base during creation. Often broken pottery was placed in a grave because Indians believed the spirit of the dead person would then be released and could travel.

Knots

Tied on bowstrings, spearhead and arrowhead lashings, snowshoes, and other items, knots were sometimes used to keep track of the days like a calendar—each knot equaled 1 day.

Knife

Made from various materials such as bone, reed, stone, wood, antler, shell, metal, or animal teeth (bear, beaver, etc.), knives were used as weapons but also creative handiwork.

L is for . . .

Linguistic Families

There are 56 related groups of American Indian languages. A few of these speech families include Iroquoian, Algonquian, Siouan, Muskogean, Athapascan, and Wakashan.

Leggings

Both men and women wore cloth or skin covering, which were often decorated with quills, beads, or painted designs, for their legs.

Lost Tribes of Israel

This historic theory has been floating around since 721 BC. The 10 lost tribes of Israel are supposedly groups of people gathered together by Sargon, the King of Assyria. Some say he cast out 10 of the 12 tribes of Israel. Many have tried to prove that the American Indians are these missing tribes!

Lowry Ruins

Probably an Anasazi ceremonial center around A.D. 1100. This 50 room pueblo is located near Cortez.

Lodge

The term for a type of Indian house that was usually a permanent dwelling. The population of a tribe was often estimated by its number of lodges.

Little Raven

Former Arapaho principal chief; first signer for the Southern Arapaho of the Fort Wise Treaty in 1861. Known as an orator. His band did not join the rest of the Arapaho at Sand Creek as he did not trust Colorado governor John Evans. Signed the treaties that established the Cheyenne and Arapaho Reservation in Indian Territory.

Land Loss

Native Americans lost their land in many ways. Conflicts with other tribes, colonization, European settlement, treaties, and removal took away Indian lands.

Lance

Spear used for hunting and war. The hunting lance had a short shaft and a broad, heavy head. The war lance was light and had a long shaft.

Lariat

These throw ropes made of rawhide, buffalo hair, or horsehair sometimes measured up to 20 feet long!

M is for . . .

Maize

Also called Indian Corn. Known as a "cereal" plant because it probably began as some form of grass. The Indians in our state figured out every possible way to use corn as a food. The only thing the white man added was the creation of "corn flakes!"

Mortar and Pestle

A two-part milling tool, with a bowl-shaped stone, plus a club-shaped stone (or wooden bowl and wooden club), used for pulverizing or grinding plants or animal matter.

Manitou Cliff Dwellings Museum

Located in Phantom Cliff Canyon; outdoor museum of reconstructed cliff dwellings depicting the life of the Anasazi.

Medicine

Medicine could be good or bad. Medicines or charms were placed in a bag by young warriors and carried at all times. Some of the roots, leaves and bark that Indians in our state used as medicine are being rediscovered and used by today's doctors!

Moccasins

Indian shoes made of animal skin.

Medicine Man

A person who got the power to heal the sick through a secret means, usually from a dream or visions.

Mesa Verde

Where early Colorado peoples, around 750 A.D., learned to shape bowls from clay and moved out of caves and into "pit houses." Today at Mesa Verde National Park you can see pueblos that have survived almost 7 centuries! Wetherill Mesa includes Step House and Long House. Chapin Mesa includes Cliff Palace, Balcony House and Spruce Tree House.

N is for . . .

Nomadic

A way of life in which people frequently moved from one location to another in search of food. "Seminomadic" people had permanent villages, but left them in certain seasons to hunt, fish, or gather wild plant foods.

Nakasinena

Division of the Arapaho that once lived around Colorado Springs. Name means "the sagebrush people."

Nation

There are many Indian nations located within the United States, such as the Cheyenne Nation. Indian nations are called nations because their governments and laws are independent of and separate from the U.S. government. The federal government must have "government to government" relations with these Indian nations, just as it would with foreign nations, like England or Spain.

November

In 1990, President George Bush approved a joint resolution designating November 1990 "National American Indian Heritage Month." Similar proclamations have been issued each year since 1994.

Names

Indian names were often changed during one's lifetime. These names could be derived from events that happened during the person's birth, childhood, adolescence, war service, or retirement from active tribal life. Some names came from dreams, some were inherited, and sometimes names were stolen or taken in revenge. Today some Indians maintain old, traditional Indian names, while others take modern names. Since settlers often did not read or write Indian languages, they recorded Indian names phonetically (as they "sounded"). Thus Indian names were often misspelled.

National Museum of the American Indian

The Smithsonian's National Museum of the American Indian on the National Mall in Washington, D.C., symbolizes a deeper understanding between America's first citizens and those who have come to make these shores their home.

Navajo

One of America's largest Native American groups. Once led a nomadic life, frequently raiding other tribes. Southern Colorado was part of their range. After acquiring the horse, they raised livestock herds, made advances in arts and crafts, and became master horsemen. Today they are world-famous for their woven blankets and rugs, baskets, silver work, and sandpainting.

O is for . . .

Old Bones

No one knows for sure when the first people came to North America, but scientists have dated bones and artifacts discovered at Clovis, New Mexico around 11,200 years old. Testing on a skeleton found on the Channel Islands, off the coast of California showed they were about 13,000 years old. And, evidence of human habitation in southern New Mexico suggests that people may have been there as far back as 38,000 years ago.

Oklahoma

In 1867, the Arapahoes and Cheyennes agreed to give up their lands in Colorado and move here.

Origins

Some scientists believe that Native Americans actually came across a land bridge between Asia and North America. They say that during an ice age thousands of years ago, the water level was much lower and people could have walked between the two continents.

Ouray

Ute chief respected by whites and Indians for trying to promote peace. In 1880, went to Washington, D.C. to negotiate a treaty where the Utes got only a narrow strip of land in southwestern Colorado. The chief soon died and never saw his people removed from the land of their ancestors.

Oil

Indians extracted oil from the many layers of fat that came with fresh bear meat. The fat was boiled down in earthen pots to produce the oil, which was stored in gourds and pots. The oil was used for cooking and even beautifying the body! Indians would mix red pigment with the oil, add the fragrances of cinnamon and sassafras, and rub it all over their bodies.

Orators

Many Indian leaders were excellent public speakers. Powerful and dramatic speakers were vital to leaders who wanted to influence their tribe. Watch for famous Indian quotations in literature and textbooks!

Office of Indian Education Programs

This is a service organization devoted to providing quality education opportunities for American Indian people. Established in the latter part of the nineteenth century to carry out the federal government's education commitment to Indian tribes, it has become the only national education system for American Indian children and adults.

P is for . . .

Powwow

The original form of the word meant "medicine man." Medicine men would often use noise motion and confusion to scare away harmful spirits and cure people. It was also a gathering to talk about political matters. Today, the powwow is an event where Indians gather to sing, perform ceremonial dances, and share cultural pride and traditions.

Pueblo Indians

Those who lived in permanent stone or adobe houses grouped in villages in southern Colorado.

Pit Houses

Built by the peoples who lived in Mesa Verde. The main part of each house was a round pit several feet deep. Above ground level, the walls and roof were built of logs plastered with earth. Later, these dwellings became more complex and were made of adobe and stone.

Paint

Indians used many natural materials to make paint, like clay mixed with oil or grease. Yellow "paint" was made with the gall bladder of a buffalo! Why did they paint their faces or bodies? Indians used paint to look scary or beautiful, to disguise themselves, or to protect their skin from sunburn or insect bites. Indians often applied red paint because it symbolized strength and success. That is why settlers often referred to the Indians as Red Men.

Pemmican

Indian food made of animal meat, which was dried in the sun, pounded together with fat and berries. The mixture was packed into skin bags and used primarily while on the trail.

Papoose

An American Indian infant aged between birth and one year is called a papoose. A papoose spent most of his or her days snugly wrapped in a kind of cradle made of skins or bark and a wooden frame that hung on the mother's back. This sturdy frame also allowed a mother to lean her papoose against a tree or rock within sight as she worked.

Picture History

Some Indians kept a record of time and important events by painting or drawing pictures or symbols on skin, bark, or stone.

Pottery

Indian pottery was made from built-up spirals of clay that were molded or paddled, or a combination of the two methods. Most pottery served as cooking vessels.

Q is for . . .

Quillwork

Indians used the quills of porcupine or birds to make a type of embroidery. Quills were dyed with juice from berries and other materials. When they were ready to be used, the quills were either mashed with teeth or softened with hot water and flattened with rocks. The quills were then laced into moccasins, shirts, pipe covers, and other items. Beads which Indians received by trading with settlers eventually replaced quillwork.

Quotation

[An Indian warrior could] "drop his body upon the side of his horse . . . screening himself from his enemy's weapons as he lies in a horizontal position behind the body of his horse with his heel hanging over the horse's back. . . . In this wonderful condition he will hang while his horse is at the fullest speed . . . [then] rising and throwing his arrows over the horse's back."

— Indian artist George Catlin's description of Comanche horsemen

Quiver

Case used to hold arrows; made of woven plant materials or animal skins.

Quarry Site

A location where Indians went for workable stone such as flint and made stone tools.

Quirt

A short riding whip with a wood, bone, or horn handle.

R is for . . .

Rain Dancing

The rain dance ceremony, performed to encourage rainfall, was common among Indian religions because good weather is vital for a successful harvest. Rainmakers were in tune with nature; there are actual reported cases of Indians producing or preventing rain!

Roots

Indians used plant roots for food, medicine, dye, baskets, cloth, rope, salt, flavoring, and just to chew!

Rattles

Indians of Colorado made rattles from bird beaks, animal hooves, bones, pods, seashells, turtle shells and other animal parts. The rattles are used in ceremonies.

Roman Nose

Member of the Crooked Lance Society, warrior group of the powerful Southern Cheyenne. His Indian name was Sauts or "Bat." He led the attack at Aricaree Fork, Colorado in 1868, when 52 scouts held off several hundred warriors. He was killed on the first day's fight.

Rawhide

Untanned animal hide. The "green" hide was stretched on the ground or over a frame. Flesh and fat were removed. The skin was dried, washed, then buried with wood ashes which made the hair come off. Used by the Colorado Indian to make drumheads, lash lodge poles, mend broken objects and in many other ways.

Reservations

The U.S. government set aside, or "reserved," land for the Indians. These reservations originally served as a sort of prison during the beginning stages of Indian removal. At that time, reservations provided the government with some control over Indian activity and residency. This land was usually considerably less desirable land than the Indians' native territories. Today's reservations are lands that are tribally held, yet protected by the government.

Red Cloud Peak, Colorado

Named after the famous chief of the Oglala Teton Sioux.

S is for . . .

Sign Language

A way for Indians to communicate with others from a tribe whose language they did not speak.

Shaman

Medicine man and spiritual leader who was supposed to have special healing power from another world.

Secret Societies

Indians had secret groups, usually organized for religious or ceremonial reasons. Each society had a purpose, such as to cure disease.

Shield

A piece of "armor" made of a rawhide-covered frame, which was carried into battle. Shields also could be decorative and religious objects. Many tribes make shields today as an art form!

Sweatlodge

Structure used for ritual purification by sweating from exposure to very hot fires or hot steam from pouring water over hot stones. Also called a sweathouse, for some tribes also doubling as clubhouses.

Stone-boiling

Cooking method by placing preheated stones into cooking vessels.

Sacred Bundles

A group of objects treasured by a tribe. They were well-guarded and often taken into battle. The items were publicly shown only on very important occasions.

Saddle

While some Indians did use saddles on their horses, most rode bareback!

Sun Dance

This ceremonial ritual was performed by many Plains Indian tribes. Annual, multi-day renewal ceremony that took place in the summer. Was an endurance test for some participants and sometimes involved the self-torture of warriors. A special lodge with a sacred pole was built, and rituals were performed by medicine men. The Arapaho call it the Offerings Lodge, and the Cheyenne call it the New Life Lodge. At one time the federal government banned the Sun Dance. Versions of the Sun Dance are still performed by the Ute today!

Signals

Indian signs made with a pony, blanket, mirror, smoke, fire-arrow or other item to communicate over long distances.

Sachem

The supreme Indian ruler of an area where there are many related tribes.

T is for . . .

Tobacco
A sacred plant early Indians used to make offering to their gods, cure diseases, bring good luck, seal agreements and bind treaties.

Treaties
Written agreements between the U.S. government and the Indians, most of which involved the Indians giving up their native lands.

Throwing Stick
A sling or grooved stick used to hurl a lance or spear. It was used by Colorado Indians before bows and arrows.

Totem
The spirit of some natural object (usually an animal) taken by an Indian, tribe or family to guard over them.

Tomahawk
A club, axe or hammer used to chop wood, drive stakes in the ground or as a weapon.

Tabequache
Division of the Utes that once lived around Los Pinos in southwestern Colorado.

Tracking
To follow a trail by finding a sign such as a broken blade of grass, a moved stone or moccasin track. Indians learned to trail as children, so that they could find food, track enemies and disguise their own signs.

Teeth
Colorado Indians hung teeth on cords to make necklaces.

Tribe
A group of Indians with shared culture, history, original territory, ancestry, social organization, and governmental structure. A tribe may contain several bands of Indians.

Tall Bull
Hereditary name among the Cheyenne. The most famous chief by this name was one of the leaders of the Dog Soldiers. Fought against the Fifth Cavalry of the U.S. Army at Summit Springs in Colorado, where he was killed in 1869. The Battle of Summit Springs was the end of the Dog Soldiers' reign of the plains.

Thunderbird
A mythological Indian figure, as well as a part of the constellations for many Indians. Thunderbird mythology is mostly different from tribe to tribe, in general either coexisting with ancestors as an actual bird, or appearing as a spiritual nature god. The Thunderbird was good to the people in either case. Much mythology ties the thunderbird with thunder, lightning and storms.

U is for . . .

U.S. Bureau of Indian Affairs

Provides public services such as law enforcement, land records, economic development, and education to Indians. Known for mismanagement and ethical problems.

U.S. Army

Many Native Americans have fought bravely for the United States Army. Many have also given their lives for a country that was not always accepting of them.

Ute Indian Museum

Located at Montrose on the site of a farm that was the last home of Chief Ouray and his wife, Chipeta. Today, you can see feather bonnets, leather garments, dance skins and other items.

U.S. Indian Schools

The Bureau of Indian Affairs operates hundreds of federal schools around the nation. Enrollment of Native American children measures in the thousands!

U.S. Indian Reorganization Act

Passed by Congress in 1934, the act authorized Indian tribes to establish and conduct their own governments, and to form businesses.

Ute

Colorado Indian tribe that became traveling traders and raiders after getting horses. Lost their lands and put on reservations in Colorado's gold rush. Revolted against the white's order to plow up the grazing lands of their horses, resulting in the Ute War. Today there are only 3 Indian reservations in Colorado, all belonging to the Ute.

Ute Mountain Tribal Park

Extensive archaeological district from the Anasazi era. You can also see ancient petroglyphs here. Near Cortez.

U.S. Indian Wars

The U.S. War Department has compiled an official list of "Indian Wars" that occurred in the United States. Over 50 wars were fought between the U.S. and the Indians during the period of 1790-1850.

V is for . . .

Vessels

Indians carried water in special gourds shaped liked bottles, called water vessels.

Village Councils

These were held in the town (council) house and occurred to discuss and decide important matters. Harmony and agreement was essential to tribal unity. Rather than vote on issues, they were discussed until everyone was satisfied. Anyone who wanted to could speak freely. Everyone did not always agree on the outcome, but everyone avoided conflict by pushing their case.

Vegetable Dyes

Indians could not buy color from the store like we can today. Instead, they created many different colors from the things they found on earth like plants, flowers, shrubs, trees, roots, and berries. They made beautiful and unique reds, oranges, yellows, greens, browns, and violets. These dyes were used for baskets, pottery, weaving, body makeup, and clothing.

Very Hungry

There were Indians who here hunters, gatherers and foragers, that often ate whatever they could find! How hungry would you have to be to eat what they sometimes ate: reptiles, larvae, and insects?

Villages

Many Colorado Indians lived in villages! Villages were formed around different clans or bands within the tribe, but could also contain different clans living together. Villages were usually permanent settlements, although semi-nomadic tribes have been known to migrate between permanent villages.

Vesperic Indians

Indian tribes located in the United States.

W is for . . .

War Bonnet
Special headdress worn into battle, often adorned with feathers.

War Pony
Horse, often painted with colorful paint and ridden into battle.

Women
Indian women in some tribes were poor and hardworking, like the men. But in some tribes, women had many rights, including becoming chief!

William Bent
Owner of Bent's Fort, the first permanent white settlement in Colorado. Indian Agent for the Cheyenne, and had an Indian wife. He worked to get Colorado Indians a fair price for their lands the whites wanted.

Whistle
Indians from Colorado made them from the wing bones of birds. The whistles made the sound of the bird the bones came from! Used to communicate, signal, sound an alarm or even flirt with a maiden!

War Club
A weapon made of stone, bone, or wood in the shape of a club.

White Man
Indians generally called them Pale Face, a name the white men themselves suggested!

War Dance
Indian braves danced this before going into battle. The dance was a way of assembling the braves and getting them to commit to the fight ahead.

XYZ are for . . .

Xenophobe

A xenophobe is someone who is afraid of foreign people, their customs and cultures, or foreign things. Many of the first European settlers were afraid of Native American cultures.

Yucca National Monument

Site of two large mounds of unexcavated rubble and earth that date back to the Pueblo Culture. Near Cortez.

Zounds!

Between 1871 and 1913, at least 98 traditional agreements between tribes and the United States were negotiated and 96 of them were ratified by Congress. Each agreement remains as law (unless changed by a later agreement)!

ZZZZZZ...

Shamans and medicine men were not the only people who had access to the spirit world. Indians believed that people could make contact with spirits every night in their dreams! Dreamers could travel back to the time of man's creation or far ahead into their own futures. They also believed that dreams contained warnings or commands from the spirits. Many tribes felt that they had to act out their dreams as soon as they awoke. If an Indian dreamed about bathing, for example, he would run to his neighbors' houses first thing in the morning, and his neighbors would throw kettles full of cold water over him.

Yuma

Indian tribe that once lived on both sides of the Colorado River. A Colorado county is named for them.

Y... Or, "Why?"

1. Why do you think Indian warriors carried charms with them? Some Indian medicines have been scientifically proven to have true healing power and are still used today. Do you think their charms had any real power to help them win battles?
2. Why do you think the American government kept relocating Indians onto reservations and then making the reservations smaller and smaller?
3. Why did Indians use items such as a pipe in ceremonies? What kinds of symbolic objects do we use in ceremonies today?
4. Why and how did Indians use natural materials in creative ways?
5. Many Indian tribes are running successful businesses on their reservations today. There is one industry that many tribes are making a lot of money at. Do you know what this is? Hint: "I'll bet you do!"

Which Famous Native American Am I?

Solve the puzzle!

Word Bank

Black Elk	Crazy Horse	Sitting Bull	Sequoia
Sacajawea	Chief Joseph	Geronimo	Pocahontas

Down

1. This Shoshone woman joined Lewis and Clark as their guide and translator and helped make the expedition a success! Hint: She has 4 "a"s in her name!
4. This man gave the Cherokee their first alphabet so that they could write. Until then, they communicated only by speaking and drawing pictures. Hint: A famous ancient tree also has the same name!
5. He was one of the fiercest of Indian warriors! He fought against white settlers in Arizona and New Mexico to keep his people from being pushed off their lands. Hint: Jump!

Across

2. A legend says that this brave Algonquian woman saved the life of Englishman John Smith. Hint: Disney produced a movie about her.
3. He fought at Little Bighorn when he was only 13! He was also a wise "shaman" who saw visions and could advise people. Hint: Part of his name is an animal with antlers!
6. He was a great Sioux warrior who won the battle against General Custer at Little Bighorn in 1876. Hint: His horse was not crazy!
7. A leader of the Lakota (Sioux) tribe who lived on the Standing Rock Reservation in North Dakota after the battle of Little Bighorn. He tried to make conditions better for his people there, so the U.S. government called him a "troublemaker." Hint: He did not sit all the time!
8. A wise and brave chief of the Nez Percé who tried to bring his people to Canada to escape war. He said, "From where the sun now stands, I will fight no more forever." Hint: His father's name was "Old Joseph."

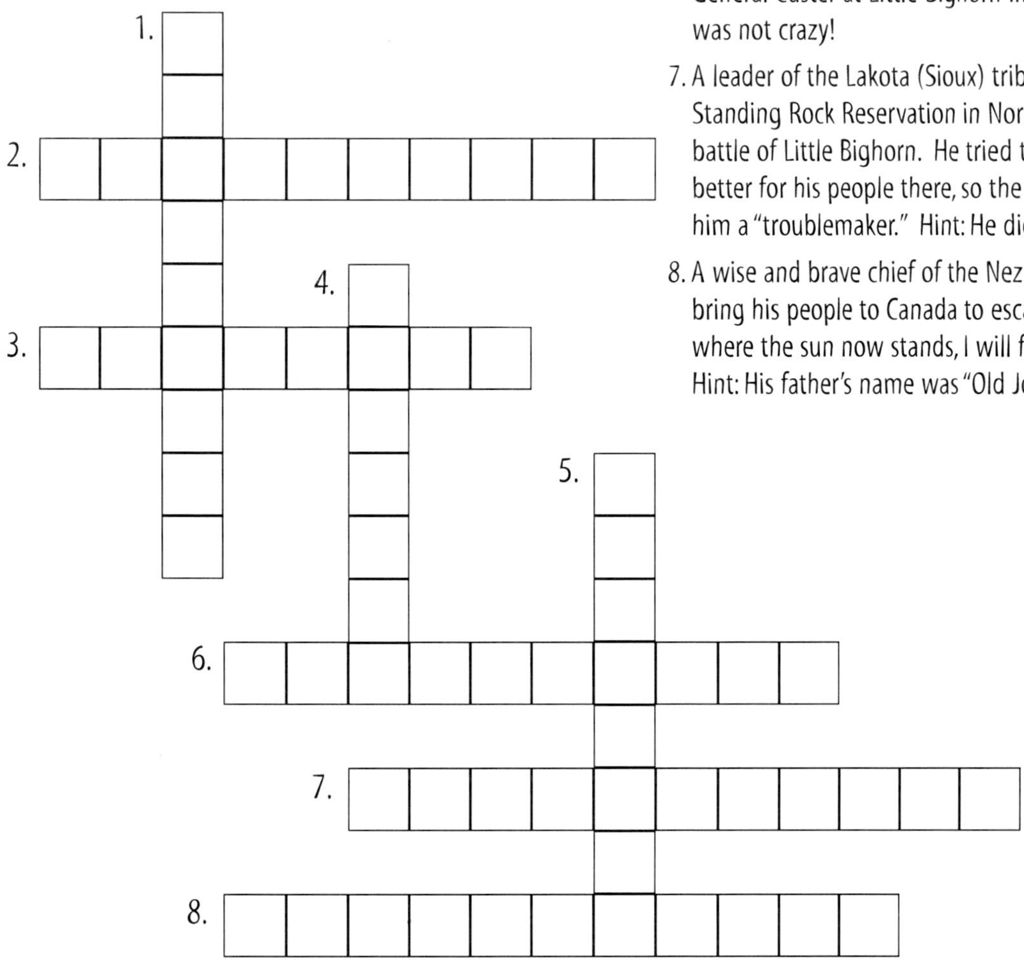

Answer Key: 1. Sacajawea; 2. Pocahontas; 3. Black Elk; 4. Sequoia; 5. Geronimo; 6. Crazy Horse; 7. Sitting Bull; 8. Chief Joseph

Different Ways for Different Indians!

North American Indian tribes are divided into different areas. In each of these areas, tribes shared common ways of living with each other. They might make similar arts or crafts, they might eat the same foods, or they might have had the same beliefs. These activities are all part of their "culture." Each area had its own culture, which was different from the tribes in all the other areas.

Below is a map of all the different groups of Indian tribes in North America. Color each area with a different color. You will see a colorful picture of how Native Americans can all be called "Indians" but still have very different cultures!

Celebration!

Powwows are big festivals where Native Americans gather to sing, dance, and eat together. It is a time to celebrate and show pride in their culture. Powwows can last from one afternoon to several days. The Indians dress in native costumes and dance ancient dances to the beating of drums.

Artists sell their arts and crafts. You might be able to buy some real Native American food cooked on an open fire. Native Americans go to powwows to be with each other, share ideas, and just have fun! Most powwows are also open to people who are not Indian. It's a great place to learn about Native American culture!

If you went to a powwow this weekend, what do you think you would see? What do you think might NOT be there? Circle the objects you think you would see at a powwow. Put an X through those you probably won't see.

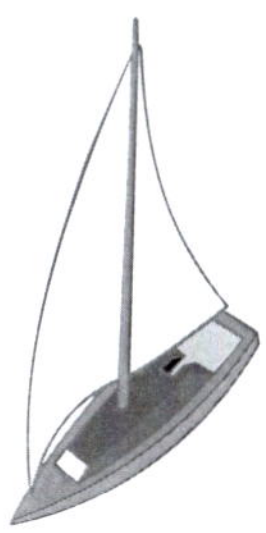

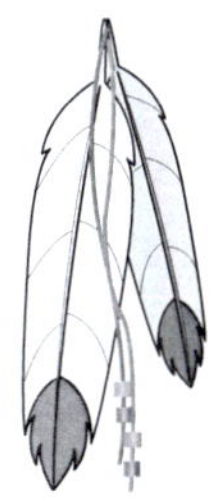

Answer Key: Circled objects are: beads, moccasins, open fire, drums, feathers, baskets, kids, food, drums, horse.

Make an Indian Weaving!

Many Native Americans used weaving to create useful things like sashes (belts), bags, mats, and blankets. They used animal hair to make yarn, and dyed the yarn with natural dyes from fruits and other plants. They also used some plant fibers, like cotton, to make weaving thread.

Weave a small Native American mat of your own. Use different colors of yarn to create a beautiful pattern in your weaving. Place a favorite object on the mat or hang it on your wall!

Prepare the "loom"

Cut a piece of cardboard 5 inches wide and 6 inches long. Along the two 5-inch sides (the "short" sides), have an adult cut slits 1/4 inch deep. These slits should be 1/2 inch apart from each other. So, on each short side you will have 9 slits.

Directions:

1. Take a long piece of yarn and bring it from the back through the first slit (the one next to the edge of the cardboard.) The end of the yarn will hang down behind the cardboard.

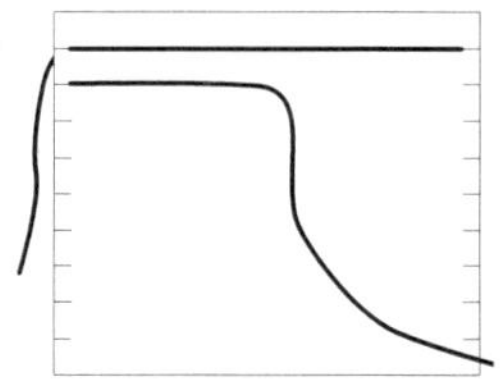

2. Bring the yarn right across the front of the cardboard to the slit opposite the one your yarn came through.

3. Now bring the yarn under the back of the cardboard and then up again through the second slit.

4. Repeat #2 and #3, until you have 9 strands of yarn across the front of your cardboard!

5. Then cut the yarn and tie the two loose ends in the back of the cardboard.

6. Take another piece of yarn and start feeding it through the 9 strands, going over one, under the next over the next, etc. When you get to the end, pull the yarn behind the cardboard and around to the front, and begin again. This time, whatever strand you went over, go under. And whatever strand you went under, go over.

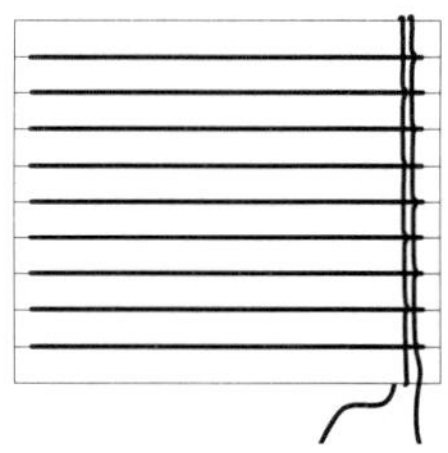

7. Repeat this pattern until the front of your cardboard in covered. Then cut the yarn in the back of the cardboard, and trim it to create a fringe for your mat!

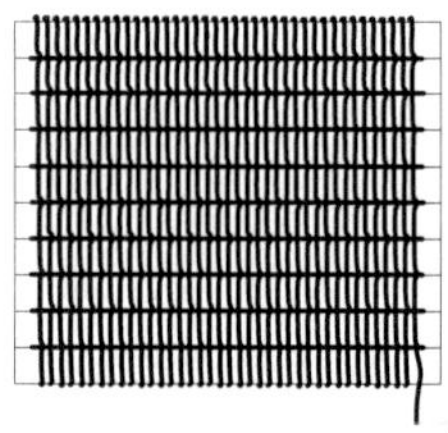

Tips:

- For a wild look, use variegated or different colored yarn!
- For a tighter mat, push the under/over strands up against the previous strands during weaving.
- To keep your mat from unravelling, tie neighboring fringe together up close to the mat.

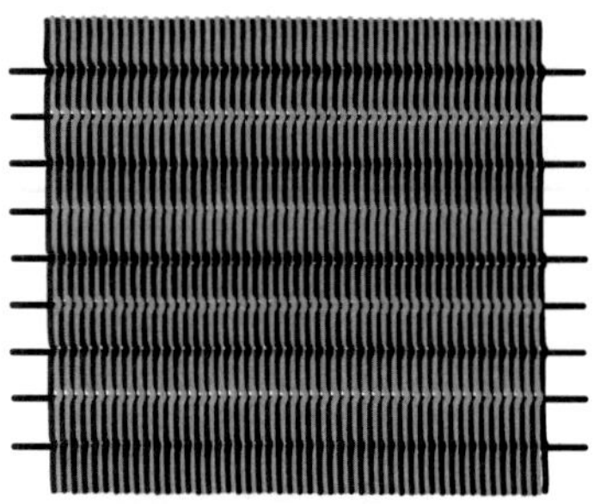

Finders Keepers?

Native Americans have many buried treasures. For hundreds of years, special objects would sometimes be buried with Native Americans, or maybe they would just be lost. Archeologists used to dig for interesting artifacts in old Native American gravesites. They would keep the Native American bones or the arrowheads, rattles, masks and other objects that they found. But this made the Native Americans feel like they were being robbed.

In 1990, the U.S. government passed a law that said that no one could look for or take these Native American objects anymore. And whoever had any already had to give them back to the people they belonged to. This is called repatriation

Help the archeologist return the artifact to a Native American.

Fast Fact

An artifact is an object that was made by people a long time ago for some useful purpose.

Busy Hands!

Before modern times, Native Americans didn't have stores where they went to buy things. They made everything they needed.

What did Indians make with their own hands? Use the Word Bank and pictures to find out!

Word Bank

blanket	moccasins	arrows	pottery	canoe
mat	food	jewelry	pouch	box

 ___ ___ ___

 ___ ___ ___ ___

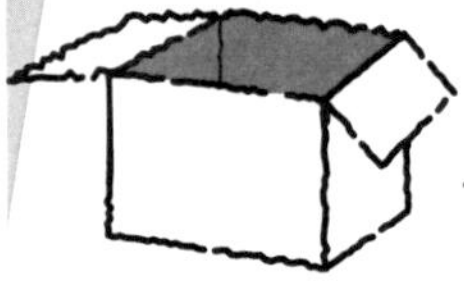 ___ ___ ___

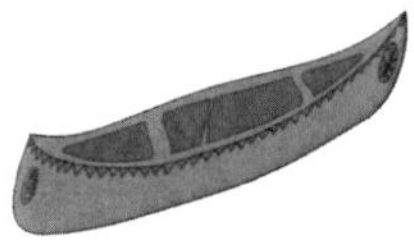 ___ ___ ___ ___ ___

 ___ ___ ___ ___ ___ ___ ___

 ___ ___ ___ ___ ___

 ___ ___ ___ ___ ___ ___ ___ ___ ___ ___

 ___ ___ ___ ___ ___ ___

 ___ ___ ___ ___ ___ ___ ___

 ___ ___ ___ ___ ___ ___ ___

American Indians Today

Beginning with the first letter of each group of letters, cross out every other letter to discover some new words. You may not have heard of these before, but you can read all about them!

1. Many Indians live on these, but many more do not!

TRYELSDEBRNVJAOTPIPOWNASX

____

2. Many Indians have been poor for a long time because for many years the government took away their lands and their ability to make a living.

TPKOOVWEBRNTXYA

____

3. Many Indians have been studying hard at school and going to college in order to earn more money. Education helps the Indians make their lives better. These Native Americans are working to become:

TSJUMCBCFEYSMSOFPUVL

____

4. This is a big term that means Native Americans have worked hard to get the U.S. government to let them rule themselves. This means that they have their own laws and make their own decisions. They are like a separate country inside the U.S.! Now, try and see if you can get your parents to give you the same thing!

TSGENLBF ***JDGEETSEWRAMCIHNUAKTYIKOTNU***

______________ ____________________________________

Fast Fact

What do Indians work as today?

- doctors
- nurses
- factory workers
- artists
- lawyers
- actors

The same kinds of jobs any American might work at!

Native Americans Move to the City!

Solve the code to discover the mystery words!

A	B	C	D	E	F	G	H	I	J	K	L	M
✷	❀	⌘	♣	➽	♥	❗	✧	✂	✆	☛	✈	✉
N	**O**	**P**	**Q**	**R**	**S**	**T**	**U**	**V**	**W**	**X**	**Y**	**Z**
✿	☆	❖	✡	✏	❦	☎	✒	✙	✖	✍	✠	✓

1. During the 1950s and 1960s, the American government paid Indians to leave their homes on reservations and move to cities to get jobs. If cities are sometimes called urban areas, then these brave Indians were called:

___ ___ ___ ___ ___   ___ ___ ___ ___ ___ ___ ___

✒ ✏ ❀ ✷ ✿   ✂ ✿ ♣ ✂ ✷ ✿ ❦

2. Many Indians chose to stay on their reservations and not move to the city. They thought that if they moved to the city, they would lose the way of life that their parents and ancestors had taught. These Indians called themselves:

___ ___ ___ ___ ___ ___ ___ ___ ___ ___ ___   ___ ___ ___ ___ ___ ___ ___

✏ ➽ ❦ ➽ ✏ ✙ ✷ ☎ ✂ ☆ ✿   ✂ ✿ ♣ ✂ ✷ ✿ ❦

3. Native Americans who moved to cities lived close to each other. They tried to keep their way of life as much as possible. They did not want to forget their religion, native art, or music. They did not want to lose their:

___ ___ ___ ___ ___ ___ ___

⌘ ✒ ✈ ☎ ✒ ✏ ➽

4. Are you afraid of heights? Many people are. The Mohawk Indians are not! Many of them work hundreds of feet above the city to build steel frames for skyscrapers. People who do this work above the city are:

___ ___ ___ ___ ___   ___ ___ ___ ___ ___ ___ ___

❦ ☎ ➽ ➽ ✈   ✖ ☆ ✏ ☛ ➽ ✏ ❦

5. Today urban Indians and reservation Indians come together to celebrate their culture. They share ideas and stories. They dance and beat drums. They make and sell Indian jewelry. During these celebrations, Indians remember how much they have to be proud of! These big parties are called

___ ___ ___ ___ ___ ___ ___

❖ ☆ ✖ ✖ ☆ ✖ ❦